582.13   Schwartz, David M.
SCH
         Among the flowers

      1000617

$13.46

W9-BAQ-805

DISCARD

AMONG THE FLOWERS

David M. Schwartz *is an award-winning author of children's books, on a wide variety of topics, loved by children around the world.* Dwight Kuhn's *scientific expertise and artful eye work together with the camera to capture the awesome wonder of the natural world.*

For a free color catalog describing Gareth Stevens Publishing's list of high-quality books and multimedia programs, call 1-800-542-2595 (USA) or 1-800-461-9120 (Canada). Gareth Stevens Publishing's Fax: (414) 225-0377.

Library of Congress Cataloging-in-Publication Data

Schwartz, David M.
    Among the flowers / by David M. Schwartz; photographs by Dwight Kuhn.
       p. cm. — (Look once, look again)
    Includes bibliographical references (p. 23) and index.
    Summary: Introduces, in simple text and photographs, the characteristics of
a variety of flowers and some of the birds and insects that need flowers to survive.
Includes the sunflower, bleeding heart, daylily, rose, bumblebee, butterfly, and hummingbird.
    ISBN 0-8368-2241-2 (lib. bdg.)
    1. Flowers—Juvenile literature. 2. Animal-plant relationships—Juvenile literature.
[1. Flowers. 2. Animal-plant relationships.] I. Kuhn, Dwight, ill. II. Title.
III. Series: Schwartz, David M. Look once, look again.
QK653.S39   1998
582.13—dc21   98-6309

This North American edition first published in 1999 by
Gareth Stevens Publishing
1555 North RiverCenter Drive, Suite 201
Milwaukee, Wisconsin 53212 USA

First published in the United States in 1997 by Creative Teaching Press, Inc., P.O. Box 6017, Cypress, California, 90630-0017.

Text © 1997 by David M. Schwartz; photographs © 1997 by Dwight Kuhn. Additional end matter © 1999 by Gareth Stevens, Inc.

All rights to this edition reserved to Gareth Stevens, Inc. No part of this book may be reproduced, stored in a retrieval system, or transmitted in any form or by any means, electronic, mechanical, photocopying, recording, or otherwise without the prior written permission of the publisher except for the inclusion of brief quotations in an acknowledged review.

Printed in the United States of America

1 2 3 4 5 6 7 8 9 03 02 01 00 99

AMONG THE FLOWERS

by David M. Schwartz

photographs by Dwight Kuhn

A SPRINGBOARDS INTO SCIENCE SERIES

Gareth Stevens Publishing

MILWAUKEE

These little yellow stars are tiny flowers. They are in the middle of a big flower head that follows the Sun.

5

A sunflower is actually
many tiny flowers.
Each little flower makes
one seed. Birds and
people eat the seeds.

How do you think the
sunflower got its name?

6

Tiny scales make this insect's wings very colorful. You cannot miss this beautiful insect when it flutters by.

A butterfly's wings are
covered with tiny scales.
They are too small to see,
but they will come off
if you touch the wings.
The scales will cover
your fingers like dust.

Do not touch a butterfly
because it needs its
scales to fly!

8

This heart-shaped flower will not be in bloom on Valentine's Day. Too bad!

This plant is called a bleeding heart. Can you see why?
Can you see other shapes in the flowers? Some people find
rabbits, a harp, and a bottle.

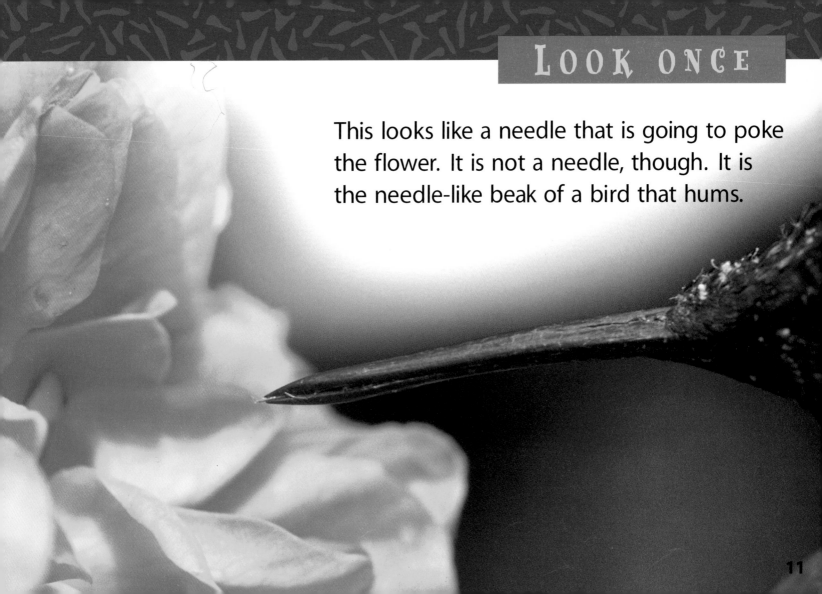

This looks like a needle that is going to poke the flower. It is not a needle, though. It is the needle-like beak of a bird that hums.

Hummingbirds drink the sweet liquid of flowers, called nectar.
Nectar gives hummingbirds the energy they need to fly.
Their wings can beat eighty times every second.
The beating wings make a loud humming sound.

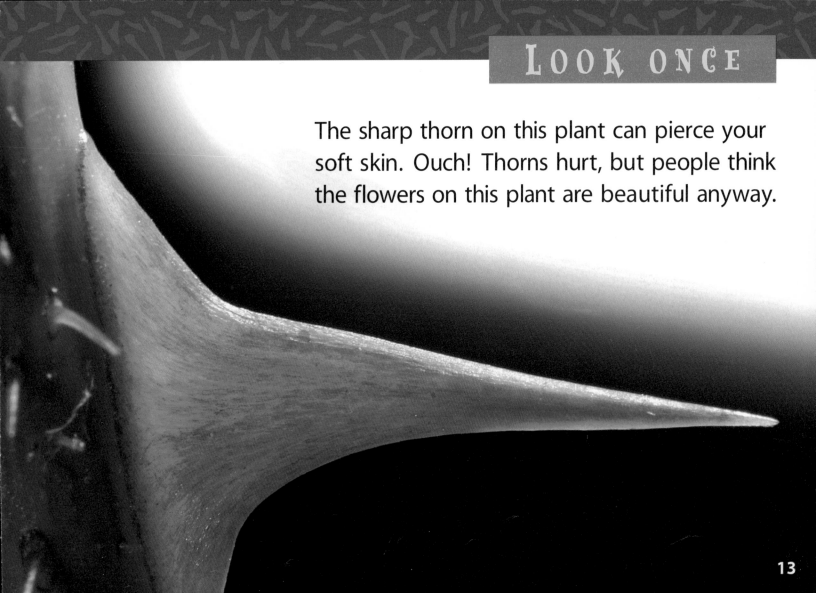

The sharp thorn on this plant can pierce your soft skin. Ouch! Thorns hurt, but people think the flowers on this plant are beautiful anyway.

Roses smell wonderful.
There are more than
twenty thousand different
kinds of roses, and they
come in almost every
color of the rainbow.
Some roses are as small
as the tip of your finger,
and some are almost
as big as your head.

This hairy black leg carries
a waxy ball of pollen.
The leg is from an insect
that is as busy as a . . .

15

...bee. Why is this bumblebee so busy? It is visiting flowers to collect pollen. Bees chew the pollen and make it into waxy balls.

Bees carry these pollen balls on their hind legs in "pollen baskets." At their nest, they feed the pollen to the queen bee and her young.

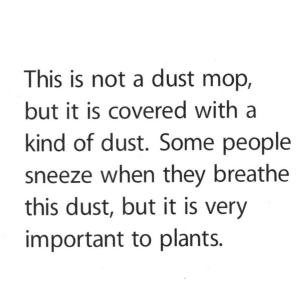

This is not a dust mop, but it is covered with a kind of dust. Some people sneeze when they breathe this dust, but it is very important to plants.

The dust is called pollen. The pollen shown here comes from a daylily. A lily needs pollen from another lily so it can make seeds. Insects and other animals carry pollen from flower to flower.

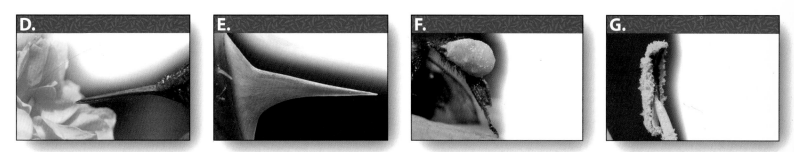

Look closely. Can you name these plants and animals?

19

LOOK AGAIN

A.

Sunflower

B.

Butterfly

C.

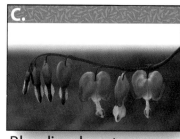

Bleeding heart

D.

Hummingbird

E.

Rose

F.

Bumblebee

G.

Daylily

How many were you able to identify correctly?

energy: the ability to act, work, and put forth effort; usable heat or electric power.

flutter: to flap and beat the wings quickly while flying or suspended in the air. Hummingbirds flap their wings as much as eighty times per second.

lily: a plant that has a tall, leafy stem and white or brightly colored flowers shaped like trumpets. Lilies grow from bulbs.

liquid: a substance that flows easily, like water or milk. Nectar is a sweet liquid produced by flowers.

nectar: a sweet liquid produced by flowers that attracts birds and bees and other insects.

pierce: to make a small hole or mark with a pointed object.

pollen: tiny, usually yellow, grains of a flower that help produce seeds. Some people are allergic to the pollen of certain plants. It makes them sneeze.

pollen basket: the smooth area on the back leg of a bee that is edged by stiff hairs and used to collect and carry pollen.

queen bee: the large female bee whose job is to lay eggs. There is only one queen bee in each hive or colony of bees.

scale (n): a small, overlapping plate on the surface of a butterfly's wing.

thorn: a sharp point growing from the stem of a plant.

waxy: covered with, or looking like, wax.

ACTIVITIES

Make Your Own Cards

After asking permission from the property owner, pick some flowers. Carefully place the flowers between two paper towels inside a book. After a few weeks, remove the flowers and arrange them on the front of a card made from construction paper. Glue the dried flower pieces onto the card. You can also decorate bookmarks or gift tags with dried flowers.

Experience Indoor Flower Power

Visit a garden center or nature center. Compare and contrast the various flowering plants on display, finding ways that they are alike and ways that they are different. What is the biggest flower you see? The smallest?

It Fits the Bill

The hummingbird has a beak that is perfect for drinking nectar out of a flower's slender blossoms. There are many different kinds of hummingbirds around the world, with beaks of different lengths and shapes. Find out more about the various types of hummingbirds by visiting your library or searching the Internet. Why are some beaks longer than others? Why are some more curved than others?

Educated Guess

Scientists make a hypothesis, or educated guess, of what they think the result of an experiment will be. What do you think will happen if you put the stem of a freshly cut white flower into some colored water? Add a few drops of food coloring or ink to water in a jar. Put the stem into the water. What happens? Have an adult help you split a flower's stem lengthwise. Put one half of the stem in one color of water and the other half in a second color. What happens?

More Books to Read

Butterflies. The New Creepy Crawly Collection (series). Graham Coleman (Gareth Stevens)
Flower. Ivan M. Anatta (Child's World)
Flowers. Terry J. Jennings (Childrens Press)
Flutter by, Butterfly. Nature Close-ups (series). Densey Clyne (Gareth Stevens)
The Nature and Science of Flowers. Exploring the Science of Nature (series).
   Jane Burton and Kim Taylor (Gareth Stevens)
What's Your Favorite Flower? Allan Fowler (Childrens Press)

Videos

Flowers. (Coronet, The Multimedia Group)
Flowers and Bees: A Springtime Story. (Encyclopædia Britannica Educational Corporation)
What Do Flowers Do? A First Film. (Phoenix/BFA Films & Video)

Web Sites

birding.miningco.com/msub1-hummers.htm
ourworld.compuserve.com/homepages/kbservices/bumble.htm

Some web sites stay current longer than others. For further web sites, use your search engines to locate the following topics: *bumblebees, butterflies, flowers, garden, hummingbirds,* and *plants.*

INDEX